The Gratitude Principle

Library and Archives Canada Cataloguing in
Publication

Sullivan, Dan, 1944-
        The gratitude principle : your future is what
you appreciate today / Dan Sullivan.

Includes index.
ISBN 1-897239-05-X

        1. Gratitude. 2. Happiness. I. Title.

BF575.G68S84 2006   158.1   C2006-905595-5

Printed in Toronto, Canada. May 2015. The Strategic Coach Inc., 33 Fraser Avenue, Suite 201,
Toronto, Ontario, M6K 3J9.

This publication is meant to strengthen your common sense, not to substitute for it. It is also not
a substitute for the advice of your doctor, lawyer, accountant, or any of your advisors, personal or
professional.

If you would like further information about the Strategic Coach® Program or other Strategic Coach® ser-
vices and products, please telephone 416.531.7399 or 1.800.387.3206. Fax: 416.531.1135. Email:
info@strategiccoach.com.

PART I:
The Gratitude Principle™.

We all love the grateful person, especially if they're talented and successful. The grateful individual is deeply appreciated, and people go out of their way to assist their progress because there is something happy and special about them. Conversely, we quickly take a disliking to the person who shows no gratitude for the opportunities, advantages, and support others have provided. We want to put obstacles in their way.

There is a fundamental principle at work here: We can achieve endless progress and success in our lives as long as we are increasingly grateful each step along the way. Lack of gratitude is one of the biggest obstacles to personal progress.

Sorry for themselves.

There are many people today, both rich and poor, who feel sorry for themselves. They look around and see others getting ahead of them. These other people seem to have so much. When they look at what they themselves have, it seems like nothing. As life goes forward, they find it more and more difficult to improve their situation. *They have no gratitude.*

Self-made.
Many others have worked hard to make themselves into successful people, but they see all this as their own doing. Nothing that other people did to help them matters in the least. They resent the suggestion that others were involved in their success. Gradually, they find themselves isolated and running out of steam. It gets harder and harder to improve. *They have no gratitude.*

Born on third base.
Still others live in advantageous circumstances and take everything for granted. Some children of wealthy parents are born on third base and think they've hit a triple. Everything is made easy for them. They never have to work hard, take risks, overcome disadvantages, or create anything new and useful; yet they have an extraordinarily high opinion of their own abilities and accomplishments. However, when these individuals are confronted with challenges that require their own skill, courage, and initiative, they falter badly. All their lives, things have worked, and now suddenly this has stopped. Somebody's to blame for this! They either become resentful and cynical—or they become deeply depressed and fearful, feeling that the whole world is going downhill. *They have no gratitude.*

Symptoms and cure.

In these three examples illustrating no gratitude, which involve envy, resentment, arrogance, alienation, complacency, cynicism, hopelessness, and depression, we see many of the symptoms of mental illness that afflict people today. Could it also be that a cure for these ailments lies in the lifelong cultivation—starting at any age—of the attitudes and skills of gratitude? Let's consider the education of children first.

Teaching gratitude as a fundamental skill from early childhood.

There is much discussion today regarding what children should be taught from the earliest age—reading, music, languages, problem-solving, computer skills, and so on. It is my contention that a person can have learned all these things and may very well be highly successful in a superficial sense, *but if they haven't learned gratitude*, they will still not be happy. And without happiness, which depends directly on the ability to be grateful, success in life means very little.

Here is my definition of gratitude:
Gratitude is an internally-generated capability that allows an individual to create and discover unlimited meaning and value in every situation and relationship in life.

Can be learned at any age by anyone.
Unlike many human abilities, it is never too late to *fully* learn and develop gratitude. The skill can be acquired at any age. I believe the reason for this is that the very structure of our brain is programmed to understand the value of gratitude. It is just that many people as children are taught by role models—parents, friends, teachers—who are themselves ungrateful.

They never see or understand the power of gratitude, so they never develop the ability. But it only needs to be awakened for it to become a lifetime tool for transforming the world around us.

Before examining what a world transformed by gratitude looks like, let's look at a central problem of modern life: the inability to deal creatively with consumerism.

PART II:
Empty and full individuals.

There are some popular views promoted by certain schools of psychology and philosophy that blame unhappiness on the emptiness and alienation of modern life. Proponents and followers of these views believe that material progress and comfort have led to increased levels of personal unhappiness. Often, the blame is put on society, with individuals being seen as helpless victims of outside forces. Inside this belief system, it becomes very difficult for an individual to generate their own happiness.

My experience has led me to a different, more personally empowering view of the world, which is captured in four basic beliefs:

One, understanding all the reasons for unhappiness will not make a person happier. It will probably make things worse.

Two, happiness is not discovered. Rather, it is uniquely created on an individual basis through the acquisition and cultivation of certain lifetime attitudes and habits.

Three, meaning and value in life do not come from outside a

person, but are created from a conscious transformation of one's outlook on daily experience.

Four, the attitudes and habits that will make each individual the happiest—and provide the greatest sense of meaning and value—are generated from the daily activity of being grateful.

With these points in mind, we can begin understanding the world we live in—*modern consumer society*—in a much more proactive way. By using these four points as guides for decision-making and action, it becomes possible to become increasingly happy in this world and to find it rich with meaning and value.

Gratification must be continually balanced by gratitude.
All consumerism is based on gratification of our senses—hearing, seeing, smelling, tasting, and touching. The more that people desire to be gratified in new ways, the greater their consumer activity. This contributes to increased economic growth and to ever-higher standards of material convenience and comfort. New technologies continually introduce new possibilities of gratification. We are now into an endlessly innovative consumer process that takes us to higher levels of material benefit. Within this process, a great

many historical evils—hunger, illness, poverty, unemployment, war, and even aging—will be dramatically decreased and even eliminated in the coming century.

That's the good news. The bad news is that none of the benefits of the consumer process guarantee anyone personal happiness or a sense of meaning and value in daily life. Indeed, the opposite may be true. Increased consumerism—without an understanding of the role of gratitude—may lead to unhappiness or, at worst, mental illness and depression. The more gratified people seek to become as consumers, the emptier they can become as human beings.

The better things become for all of us, the unhappier many of us become as individuals.

No gratitude, no meaning.
The process of consumer gratification always starts on the outside of an individual. It is something new that they take in from the world.

To balance this, there must be a process just as powerful that starts on the inside. There must something new that goes out to the world. That's the way everything in nature works—as part of a reciprocal, interactive process.

We are at the very center of natural evolution.

Just having the first process of consuming without the second—creating—is what quickly depletes life of all meaning. It is what makes people intensely unhappy. They are contradicting the most fundamental of natural laws. Because gratification occurs on a psychological and emotional level, they suffer psychologically and emotionally.

There is no cure on the outside; it can only come from within.

Gratitude is an internally-generated process that balances the power of consumption. Out of gratitude come creative activities in our lives that provide us with meaning and value.

PART III:
Lifetime of appreciation.

When we say that we are grateful, something fundamentally important is going on: We are *appreciating* something in a new way. What does "appreciate" mean?

My definition is *to increase the value of something.*

When we appreciate something, we are giving it a new value it did not have before. This, in fact, is how everything in the world acquires its value. Someone appreciates it. It always begins with a specific individual. Until someone appreciates a particular thing, event, situation, or relationship, there is no value in it. All value in the world is created by individuals appreciating something. The activity of gratitude is what allows this process of appreciation to begin.

Value and meaning.
With increased value comes greater meaning. The things we value or appreciate the most also have the greatest meaning. Value and meaning in the world, then, are totally created by appreciation.

It's crucial to understand how gratitude or appreciation

creates value and meaning—that it all comes from inside
each individual. Many people do not believe this. In fact,
they believe just the opposite. For them, value and meaning
come from the outside. It becomes someone else's respon-
sibility to do the creating. They are simply consumers of life.

Proactive and reactive gratitude.
Many other people are grateful—but only when others do
something uniquely special for them. Or when they uniquely
benefit from special circumstances and advantages. But
it must be uniquely about them. That's *reactive gratitude*,
which is very important. It's important to recognize and
acknowledge things that uniquely benefit us.

An exponentially greater power, however, lies in *proactive
gratitude*, where you recognize something special that is not
obvious to others. In proactive gratitude, you take something
that is taken for granted by everyone else and spotlight it. In
proactive gratitude, you point out the uniqueness of things
that others have seen as ordinary.

In proactive gratitude, you bring to prominence things
that have been invisible—things that no one else saw
until you gave them greater value and meaning.

Principles of proactive gratitude.

Proactive gratitude is about appreciating everything in the world around you. It is not initiated by something special the world first does for you, but rather by something special that you first do for the world. Every time you do it, new value and meaning are created in the world—not only for yourself, but for others. Every time you do it, your ability to create value grows.

Proactive gratitude allows you to enter into a special relationship with the world—one that continually grows in value, meaning, and happiness.

The ten principles on the following pages show you how to establish and cultivate proactive gratitude in yourself over a lifetime.

Proactive Gratitude 1:

Appreciating the fact that you have life and can reflect on it.

People who have had near-death experiences report that afterward, they have an overwhelming appreciation for life. From the moment they come back, they see each day's experiences as deliciously precious.

Alternatively, think of the many people who are bored, envious, resentful, angry, or depressed. They have this magical thing called life all around them and within them, and they fail to see the value in it. They have a marvelous brain that can think, remember, and imagine, and they take it for granted. They have senses that enable them to see, hear, taste, smell, and touch—and the capacity to be conscious of all these sensations—but this means nothing to them. Life goes by quickly, its wonders unnoticed.

Take time each day to appreciate that you're alive. Start with just a minute and extend it until you can do 15.

Proactive Gratitude 2:
Appreciating the power of the smallest things.

Many people spend their lives yearning for the Big Moment. It's like actors who live only for the Academy Award, athletes who are obsessed with the Gold Medal, politicians who lust after the Ultimate Office. Others want the Perfect Mate, the Dream House, or the Big Payday.

These are the only things they appreciate in life. Unless they can achieve their Big Moment, life is meaningless to them. Nothing short of the ultimate will provide any happiness. In the Big Moment lies the secret power that will totally transform their lives. Once the Big Moment occurs, everything will be magical. The truth is, there *is* magic in life, but it lies in the smallest moments. Those who focus only on the Big Moment miss all of these little ones where self-transformation continually takes place.

Big Moments do occur in life, but they are a bonus reward for continually appreciating the power of the smallest things.

Each day, identify and appreciate five of the smallest things that make the biggest difference in your life.

Proactive Gratitude 3:
Appreciating the infinite value that lies in the world outside of yourself.

From a newborn baby's perspective, everything exists only to satisfy their needs. Nothing outside themselves has any value except to make them feel comfortable and well-fed. Babies grow physically into children and adolescents, and then into adults. The possibility also exists for them to grow psychologically and emotionally. Physical growth depends largely on genetic programming. Psychological and emotional growth, however, are a matter of individual choice. There are many so-called adults who avoid this choice and relate to the world as if they were still babies.

True adulthood occurs to the degree that we appreciate the infinite value that exists in the world outside ourselves. The world does not exist for our individual benefit or welfare. It is a marvelous place that was here before we arrived and will be here after we go.

Each day, appreciate that you're only a short-term visitor on the planet. Be the best possible guest while you're here.

Proactive Gratitude 4:
Appreciating the infinite variety of abilities in other people and utilizing them.

You are the center of your own universe, and you are equipped with remarkable abilities. The world is a different place simply because you're here. You can make a significant difference for the better in the lives of many other people while you're here.

There's a catch to all of this, however. Your own abilities will do you good, and do good for others, only to the degree that you're able to appreciate the abilities of other people.

Here's a fundamental truth: Throughout life, our individual abilities have meaning and value only in teamwork. Only by combining our abilities with those of others can we utilize our unique gifts. The more we appreciate the infinite variety of abilities in other people, the more our own abilities become useful.

Each day, appreciate someone else's Unique Ability®. Combine it with your own.

Proactive Gratitude 5:

Appreciating the opportunities you have right now and taking advantage of them.

A drowning man refuses help three times. First a lifeguard comes, then a boat, and finally a helicopter. Each time, he says, "God will save me." In the end, he drowns. When he gets to Heaven, he is outraged and shouts at God, "Why didn't you save me?" God replies, "I tried. First I sent you a lifeguard, then a boat, and finally a helicopter. What more do you want?"

Just as some people are looking for the Big Moment, others are looking for the Big Opportunity that is going to "save" their lives. Countless little opportunities appear to them every day, but they ignore all of them. They want the big one, and nothing else will do. But the fact of life is this: Recognizing opportunity is actually a lifetime skill that requires constant practice. Big opportunities only come to those who continually appreciate and take advantage of all the little opportunities available to them.

Each day, appreciate one opportunity that you have to make progress. Take advantage of it immediately.

Proactive Gratitude 6:
Appreciating who your greatest teachers are and learning from them.

A Zen master was silent as he poured tea for a student who was talking incessantly about his need for enlightenment. Suddenly, the student stopped. "Master, the cup is overflowing!" The master nodded and smiled, "Yes, just like your mind. You seek enlightenment. First you have to be quiet and create some space."

The world around us is filled with great teachers, but our minds have to be open to learn from them. Again, it is characteristic of a consumer society that people have busy minds seeking constant gratification. They are looking for self-knowledge and wisdom, but what they get is disappointment and dissatisfaction.

Learning requires proactive gratitude. It is only when we stop and appreciate a particular quality in another person, and acknowledge it, that we are able to learn. The greater our gratitude, the greater our learning. We continually acquire for ourselves those qualities that we most appreciate in others.

Each day, appreciate one teacher in your life and learn a new lesson.

Proactive Gratitude 7:
Appreciating what your central values are.

The word "brainwashed" describes individuals who give control of their minds to authority figures. This occurs in totalitarian countries, in prison camps, in cults, and in large crowds. Brainwashing techniques can be very sophisticated, but they don't always work. It has been discovered that individuals with strong personal value systems are impervious. By the same token, people lacking a value system are very vulnerable—especially if they are young.

A personal value system is a set of conscious, permanent standards at the core of our thinking, against which we measure everything else. The people who have the strongest value systems are also those who are the most grateful. They have a keen sense of what has the greatest meaning. They know what they value and what they don't. They cannot be overwhelmed by manipulative techniques. Their thinking, communication, and behavior are impervious to others' attempts to control them.

Each day, appreciate something that is a central value for your entire life.

Proactive Gratitude 8:
Appreciating who you want to become.

Here is a prediction about your future: You will constantly be shaped by what you appreciate in life. If you appreciate the most admirable people, the most beautiful things, and things that have the greatest value, then that is what you will become yourself.

If you value something that is very limited and exclusive, that shuts you away from other people and experiences, then that's the kind of person you will become.

Our lives are constantly shaped by what we appreciate most.

The question is: What kind of person do you want to become? Then, what must you be grateful for to become that person? Look again at the previous seven gratitude principles. You will see that making these appreciation activities a part of your life will clearly define who you are going to be.

Each day, appreciate one thing that represents who you want to become.

Proactive Gratitude 9:
Appreciating how you yourself want to be appreciated.

The Golden Rule says, "Do unto others as you would have them do unto you." This raises a question: What do you want others to do unto you? For my part, I want others, first and foremost, to appreciate me for the following qualities: extraordinarily useful, deeply caring, very insightful, and endlessly innovative.

This realization dictates what I am grateful for in other people. I am increasingly appreciative of others who are useful, caring, insightful, and innovative. The more that I acknowledge these qualities in others, the more I am acknowledged for them in myself.

It's a reciprocal process—an upward spiral of appreciation, acknowledgment, and self-growth. Anyone who chooses to can experience this process. The Golden Rule becomes a dynamic daily principle when it is understood as starting with proactive gratitude.

Each day, appreciate and acknowledge in someone else one specific quality that you yourself want to be appreciated for.

Proactive Gratitude 10:

Appreciating how you can handle ever-greater success.

Rock stars, movie stars, and athletes: We've all heard stories of those who tried to go too far too fast, and crashed. Most people can handle only a limited amount of success in their lives. It has nothing to do with their abilities, but rather with their attitudes. What stops people at a certain level is a lack of proactive gratitude. They can't go any further or higher successfully because they lack an appropriate amount of gratitude. Thus, their achievements have no meaning.

The lifetime habit of proactive gratitude, on the other hand, continually creates a positive zone in front of us that allows us to achieve continually greater success. We have already made each new achievement safe for ourselves—by our increasing sense of appreciation. We can strive for any level of success in our lives because we know that our proactive gratitude guarantees that our success will have profound meaning.

Each day, use appreciation to prepare a positive zone for greater success.

PART IV:
The Gratitude Civilization.

Civilizations rise and fall. Everybody knows the stories of societies that seem to have had everything going for them, and then, for some mysterious reason, lost their direction and dynamism.

Historians talk about a loss of leadership. Religious leaders talk about a loss of morality. Economists talk about a loss of productivity. In these civilizations, material progress slowed down and stopped. Creativity declined and decadence set in. The structures of society—government, business and commerce, religious and educational institutions, the military, the police, communities, neighborhoods, and families—became fragmented, inefficient, and corrupt. Individuals in large numbers lost their sense of confidence and security. It's an old story that has been repeated in all ages in every part of the world.

Fundamental reason for decline.
To understand why civilizations and societies decline, it makes sense to study why individual human beings decline.

The same principles and processes are at work. If we can understand the latter, we can understand the former.

Individual human beings lose their sense of direction and dynamism as their ability to appreciate life is diminished. This occurs through the activity of consumption.

Consumption of what? Consumption of anything—food, drink, sex, comfort, convenience, safety, security, entertainment, excitement, progress, achievement, power, status, celebrity, and control. Everything that human beings strive for.

When the well-off are unhappy.

All forms of consumption demand appreciation, without which there is no value or meaning. The most materially well-off individuals often face the greatest challenge in remaining appreciative for all they have. Thus, they frequently suffer the greatest loss of meaning and value. Once they lose their ability to appreciate, none of their success brings them happiness.

Those with the greatest wealth, position, and power are the leadership class in every society. Everyone else looks to them for direction. When they experience a loss of meaning and value, their unhappiness spreads to everyone. The decline of a society always starts at the top, when those who are the most successful begin to feel the least satisfaction.

Individual gratitude continually revitalizes societies.
People are always searching for the factors that will guarantee the continued vitality and progress of their societies. Many factors are necessary, but one is crucial. Unless proactive gratitude is continually replenishing the overall supply of appreciation, none of the other factors will matter in the long run.

The fate of every human society, then, depends upon the degree to which the majority of individuals have acquired the daily attitude and habit of proactive gratitude.

PART V:
The 21-Day Gratitude Focus™.

Habits of any kind are established through the repetition of a specific activity over a period of time. Twenty-one days is usually considered the minimum duration. When you repeat something daily over a three-week period, the activity begins to feel natural, and it's easy to continue doing it. If we look at making gratitude into a daily habit, only when the activity of being grateful becomes automatic daily behavior is its full power achieved.

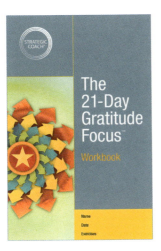

The habit workbook.

There are three tools for The Gratitude Principle™: the mini-book you are reading, an audio CD recording, and *The 21-Day Gratitude Focus*™ workbook.

In this workbook, you can establish proactive gratitude as a habit in your life through a daily exercise repeated over a three-week period. From the very first day, you will notice an increased awareness of, and sense of meaning and value from, even the smallest things you appreciate in your daily life.

PART VI

The Strategic Coach® Program.

New times require new kinds of education. The microchip revolution is vastly increasing entrepreneurial and consumer activity in global society. This is putting unbearable strains on traditional educational systems, which were designed for simpler societies where people had fewer choices.

The traditional emphasis has been on bringing individuals into lifetime conformity with inflexible agrarian and industrial institutions. The new emphasis is on enabling people to be flexible, adaptable, innovative, and responsive in a world of changing institutions. *The Gratitude Principle* is a tool that enables individuals to thrive in this world.

Lifetime program for achieving greater simplicity, balance, and focus.
The Gratitude Principle is just one of many Knowledge Products and programs provided by Strategic Coach®—an organization dedicated to transforming the whole basis of education through the teaching of entrepreneurial knowledge, attitudes, skills, and habits. Thousands of entrepre-

neurs, their families, and their support teams are presently taking advantage of programs designed to bring greater simplicity, balance, and focus into their lives.

Further information.
For further information on Strategic Coach® programs and Knowledge Products, phone **416.531.7399** or **1.800.387.3206**. Or visit our website at ***www.strategiccoach.com***.